They Absolutely Want to Write

Lesson Plans for Teaching
the Heart and Soul of Narrative Writing

By Marjie Bowker

With Assistance from Ingrid Ricks

They Absolutely Want to Write
Lesson Plans for Teaching the Heart and Soul of Narrative Writing

Cover design by Sue Vilushis

ISBN: 978-0-9908504-0-3

Book layout by Hydra House
www.hydrahousebooks.com

By Marjie Bowker
With Assistance from Ingrid Ricks

For more information, visit: www.WriteToRight.org

TABLE OF CONTENTS

Foreword   4

Why We Started This Program   5

What Students Are Saying   7

Helping Students to Identify and Write their Stories   8

Suggested Schedule for Teaching This Unit   11

Common Core State Standards: Narrative Writing   13

Definitions   14

Narrative Scenes Using SCEDS   15

Scene Construction Elements   16

Writing Prompts   17

Pre-writing Lesson: Broken Necks and Blank Minds   18

SCEDS Lesson Plans   19

Scene Construction Lesson Plans   40

Transformations   54

Our Books   57

About Marjie Bowker   58

About Ingrid Ricks   58

FOREWORD

Using the power of students' stories, Marjie Bowker and Ingrid Ricks have created a rigorous and engaging curriculum that increases self-efficacy and resiliency, teaches higher order thinking skills, touches students' hearts and souls, and transforms as it informs, all with an eye on the Common Core State Standards.

If you are looking for a curriculum designed to give students voice, this is it. After seeing the transformations in their students at Scriber Lake High School in Edmonds, Washington, they created this wonderful gift so others could have the same life-changing experiences.

Use it to teach, to inspire and most of all, to enjoy!

Cal Crow, Ph. D.
Center for Learning Connections
Center for Efficacy and Resiliency
Edmonds Community College

***

This writing project has transformed the lives of Scriber Lake students. It has freed the writers from burdens of the past and has enabled them to move on with their lives. It has also changed the lives of the students who have witnessed the courage of their peers and who desired the end result of freedom for themselves.

Even though I interact with these students on a daily basis, reading their stories has given me a depth of understanding for who they are—what they've been through and their resiliency. It makes me want to do everything I can to help them realize their dreams and goals so that they can have the futures they deserve.

The curriculum developed by Marjie Bowker and Ingrid Ricks has captured even the most reluctant writers, inspiring them to revise draft after draft of their stories. The skills they have learned has also enabled them to gain confidence in writing overall and, as a result, many of them achieved success on the writing standards required by Washington State.

I highly recommend this study guide as a tool for educators who want to make a difference in their students' lives.

Kathy Clift
Principal, Scriber Lake High School
Edmonds, Washington

WHY WE STARTED THIS PROGRAM

A Note From Ingrid Ricks

It was my own struggle with the pain I'd carried inside of me for years—followed by my ultimate decision to write and publish my memoir—that made me understand the life-changing power of personal storytelling.

I'd tried to write my memoir, *Hippie Boy: A Girl's Story*—about my childhood struggles to escape an abusive stepfather and the extreme religion and poverty at home—for more than a decade. But the emotions bottled inside me were so painful that I cried every time I opened my computer to write. I decided it was easier just to keep the hurt safely tucked away.

Then, in late January 2004, I was diagnosed with Retinitis Pigmentosa, an incurable degenerative eye disease that is slowly stealing my eyesight. In my quest to save my vision, I sought treatment from a doctor who focuses on whole body health. He kicked off my appointment by asking me to tell him about my childhood. Within minutes, I was sobbing.

The doctor told me it was clear I was carrying around a huge negative energy charge over something that happened so many years ago. Then he added, "If you don't think that carrying this inside of you is impacting your physical health, you're crazy."

The idea that holding onto the anguish from all those years ago could actually be causing me to go blind was a huge wake up call for me. I finally decided to confront my emotions and write my book, and discovered the immense healing power and validation that comes from getting the words out on paper. I also started openly sharing my story through essays and podcasts and discovered something else: that I wasn't alone in my experiences and that by sharing my story with the world, I was making connections and giving others a voice.

Even before publishing Hippie Boy, I knew I wanted to use my story to help teenagers who were struggling with similar issues to reclaim their power and move on with their lives. So when Marjie Bowker contacted me about using my book, I felt like I was being handed a huge gift.

What started as a month-long unit that used Hippie Boy as a guide to help Marjie's students find their voice and power by writing their personal stories has since turned into a comprehensive writing program. Our collaboration has so far led to three published student story collections and a life-changing experience for the student authors involved. It has led to the launch of our youth storytelling organization, WriteToRight.org, and a joint commitment to share this program with educators and mentors so more youth can experience the transformational power of personal storytelling.

A Note from Marjie Bowker

Making my students into published authors was not on my mind in the fall of 2011 when I first read Ingrid Ricks' memoir; I was just happy to find a book that I knew they would love. But when I learned the story behind Ingrid's story—that it wasn't until she gave herself permission to write her story and share it with others that she was able to let go of the pain from her childhood– I knew my students deserved that same opportunity.

Ingrid started coming into my English classes to discuss *Hippie Boy* and to ask one question of my students: "What is your story?" And despite the issues that were constantly interfering with their education—homelessness, poverty, abuse and drug and alcohol issues—they became fully engaged in answering that question.

Today, as a result of our partnership, we have published three story collections: *We Are Absolutely Not Okay, You've Got it All Wrong*, and *Behind Closed Doors: Stories from the Inside Out*. We have seen individual lives, our school and our connection to the community transform. And we have watched our students become writers—many of whom had no previous confidence, or interest, in writing. These students, and their books, are proof that most students absolutely want to write.

Relevance used to be my biggest concern as a teacher; now, however, my students read their stories publicly every chance they get: in front of their peers, at other schools, at local Rotary and Kiwanis Club meetings, at local bookstores and conferences. Last fall we adapted three stories for the stage in a partnership with Seattle Public Theater, and Edmonds Community College chose *You've Got it All Wrong* as their "Community Read" for the 2014-15 school year. My students now view themselves as participants in a universal dialogue—participants who are making a difference in other people's lives.

This curriculum, which adheres to the Common Core State Standards for Narrative Writing, is the product of Ingrid's and my journey together, helping students to identify their stories and guiding them through multiple drafts to make every detail count. What I have learned through this process is that all students have stories to tell, and that struggling writers need a different, personal and engaging approach to inspire them.

Now, at Scriber Lake High School, we write our own stories. We hope that this guide will help you and your students enter into that dialogue along with us.

WHAT STUDENTS ARE SAYING

Aydan Dennis, 14

Writing my story helped me because it allowed me to release pent-up frustration without hurting others, and lifted a weight off my shoulders. It helped me to reveal other feelings I had about what I wrote, and helped me to realize that it's okay to share this story with others.

Tattiyana Fernandez, 17

Writing my story has been a huge achievement for me! It honestly is the best thing I could have done. It has helped me overcome so many of my problems, because until then I thought I was the only one who struggled with abandonment. Knowing that my deepest story can help someone is the best feeling in the world to me.

EmmaSariah Jensen, 14

Writing my story helped me get all of my feelings out because I've never told anybody about how and who I was raised by. I feel so relieved to finally express the emotions I've held in so long.

Vasilly Karpinskiy, 14

The way writing my story helped me: well, I definitely did lose a lot of stress and now that a few people know, they are helping me get over it.

Michael Coffman, 14

Writing my story helped me let go of what happened and took away a lot of anger and resentment.

Shelby Asbury, 15

Writing my own story had its pros and cons. Although writing it helped me sort through emotions that I needed to deal with, it brought up memories I didn't want to face. In the long run it helped me because getting my story out helped me get over my fear of my abuser. Writing my story helped me heal a little faster. I cried a couple of times while writing it, and sometimes writing ruined my whole entire day. But to this day it's helping me because I got everything I've been holding in out.

HELPING STUDENTS TO IDENTIFY AND WRITE THEIR STORIES

The overall goal of this curriculum is to help students identify the stories they want to tell and then guide them through the scene-writing process by using techniques that appeal to their senses.

Our opening question is always "What is your story?" Many can answer this immediately, while some begin by saying that they don't have a story. However, as soon as they read stories from *We Are Absolutely Not Okay, You've Got it All Wrong* and *Behind Closed Doors: Stories from the Inside Out*, a light switches on inside of them.

These stories cover issues that are common in many students' lives: abandonment, divorce, poverty, power struggles, abuse and feelings of helplessness. By using these and then incorporating related questions as writing prompts, students quickly begin to identify their own personal experiences. Overall, students appreciate the "no specific prompt" approach. "It's up to you what story you are going to tell" works a lot better than "Write about a life-changing experience" because of the freedom it allows.

What we've discovered is that when given a guide to follow and an opportunity to share, students become engaged with their hearts and souls, and narrative writing no longer feels like work to them.

Writing "In Scene"

It's a big challenge to get students to narrow their stories into just one scene and to write it in the moment—to "show" instead of "tell" the story. Many tend to want to write about a string of events that happened over a long period of time.

To help students understand the concept of a "scene," we read stories from our student books and then discuss how much real time was involved in each one (in addition to all of the other topics that spring from them). All of our published writers worked hard to narrow their stories down to be told in-the-moment, so most of them take place in under a half an hour – some within just minutes. Some scenes include flashbacks to help deepen the story arc, but they are placed within the real time of the event that is happening.

We also place a high importance on individual student/teacher conferences (about ten-minutes in length) to help students visualize the scene before they begin to write. Soon we hear students asking each other, "Does this take place in under a half an hour?" If the answer is "no," then they might brainstorm how the insertion of a flashback would help focus the story.

Another constant discussion involves how "painting" the setting, characters, dialogue, emotions and sensory details (SCEDS) into the story will slow it down in order to invite readers into the experience. I repeatedly remind my students of the "Broken Necks, Blank Minds" activity because it helps them to remember that they are transferring a unique experience into the mind of a person who has no concept of what actually happened. Sometimes they ask to do this activity again for an active break from writing because they enjoy it so much.

SCEDS (Setting, Character, Emotion, Dialogue, Sensory Detail) Lesson Plans:

Before any formal scene-writing takes place, I make sure my students have been given many opportunities to practice writing "in scene."

The SCEDS lessons are designed to remove obstacles for reluctant writers by providing them with the building blocks necessary to construct descriptions of characters, settings, emotions and dialogue through the use of sensory details. Once they have the words, their ideas will flow freely. Students respond well to visual cues and quickly engage with their emotions—and these lessons invite them to do so. I have been using these techniques in my classroom for the past four years and cannot recall many refusals to participate; usually, even my least confident writers will become engaged and share their writing with the class. Most of the examples included in the SCEDS lessons are written by ninth graders – most of whom have had little success within the school system.

When students are ready to begin writing their scenes (after practicing with the basic SCEDS lessons), I usually start the process by having them use the "Your Narrative Scene – SETTING" chart to help them to write themselves into the real-time setting of their story. Once they are in-the-moment, they will usually stay there.

Although the focus is on the use of visuals, adding other sensory experiences will enhance them even further; when you can, add sounds, tastes, textures and scents. The more students engage with their senses, the more engaged they will be with writing.

Free-Writing in Response to Stories and Prompts:

Throughout this process, allow time for students to free-write their responses to stories and/or prompts; after completing the readings they are usually full of connections, so try to utilize that energy while it's at a high level.

I require between a half and a whole page of writing for each free-writing session (usually around 10-15 minutes). I have no rules for this, other than "write." I don't grade them, except for quantity, and I usually comment on them and suggest stories that spring from a portion of what they've written—often the real stories are hidden somewhere in the rambling. The most honest writing usually comes from the time that I allow them to "free write" in class.

The Formal Narrative Scene Assignment:

After reading scenes out loud from our student books and discussing them ("What did this writer do well? How did he or she "paint" this scene to make it come alive? How did the structure work in real time?"), practicing writing techniques through use of the SCEDS, many free-writes, and our ten-minute student/teacher conferences, students are practically begging to begin writing their scenes. As mentioned above, beginning with the "Your Narrative Scene – SETTING" chart will set them on the right path.

After the "first final draft" (what I call it), we work on the blending techniques and structural elements so they can be applied to their second and third drafts. (Suggested schedule included later.)

Assessment

I use the Common Core State Standards Narrative Writing Rubric to assess the formal narrative scene assignment:

http://www.schoolimprovement.com/docs/Common%20Core%20Rubrics_Gr9-10.pdf

Considerations Regarding Students' Stories:

I am very fortunate to have a competent counseling staff at my disposal; students know that if they write about a traumatic event in my class, they will be connected with an appropriate professional. If I could not depend on this support, I would hesitate to invite this type of honesty—it's a lot of responsibility, and I am not a counselor. However, over and over again, the act of objectifying these experiences through writing creates a community of understanding made up of strong individual voices. Many students express that this is the most surprisingly effective "therapy" they have ever experienced.

Some begin the writing process saying, "I'm just going to write this for myself." Some of these students change their minds and proceed to the publishing phase, while some who intend to publish decide against that step in the end. We let them set their own rules and view ourselves as guides for the process.

We also offer the choice of using a pen name. One student was afraid of gang retaliation the first year, but the second year he was ready to use his real name. Another was still in the home where her abuse scene occurred and waivered over this decision. In the end she decided to use it so that the truth of what happened was really told. Each student must consider the consequences of making a story public, and must be guided well in making that decision.

We encourage students to communicate honestly with their parents about the content of their stories (and, of course, we have students and parents sign waiver forms); however, often that is the most difficult conversation to have and it doesn't always happen.

At our first book release party, a parent approached me and said, "You know more about my daughter than I do. I hope you are prepared to provide the counseling we need over this." Her comment shook me, and I told her that our counseling staff would be happy to set an appointment with the two of them. A few days later, she told me that she and her daughter had been able to discuss her story in the past week and that they had never before shared such open communication. She admitted to feeling exposed by the story, but in the end, she expressed gratitude for the exposure because of the good it did their relationship.

When I first started this endeavor, I was uneasy about the responsibilities involved. But now I know that the benefits far outweigh the trouble. Students who desire the freedom that comes from getting their stories out and who are courageous enough to initiate that process are the reward for all the work it requires to facilitate the process.

Students as Teachers

The most rewarding part of this process is when students begin conferencing with each other on their own time, asking for and offering advice regarding how to clarify each other's stories. My students are now helping to teach these concepts in the classrooms and seminars where they present their stories; they have come full circle and are now teaching others as they continue to strengthen their own writing skills.

SUGGESTED SCHEDULE FOR TEACHING THIS UNIT

Part One: Identify Stories

Read scenes written by other student writers, free-write responses, hold ten-minute conferences.

Ask students: "What is your story?" or "What are your stories?" "Which one do you want to tell and how do you want to tell it?"

When your students have identified their stories, move on to Part Two:

Part Two: Practice Writing and Transfer Skills to Actual Scenes for Pre-Writing

Suggested Order of Lesson Plans:

1. **Pre-writing Lesson: Broken Necks/Blank Minds.**

    Establishes a general mindset regarding the transference of a unique story from one person to another and the necessity to "paint" it well into the other person's mind.

2. **SCEDS Lesson One – Writing with Sensory Detail.**

    Establishes the use of sensory detail writing in-the-moment (for all of the writing to come).

3. **SCEDS Lesson Two: Setting – Painting a Place with Words.**

    This lesson presents writers with compelling settings that are fun to imagine and write about.

4. **SCEDS Lesson Three: Character – Painting a Portrait with Words.**

    This lesson Invites writers to recognize many facets of character description.

5. **SCEDS Lesson Four, Emotional/Physical Response.**

    This lesson elicits the most heart-and-soul writing because it is emotion–based. It's interesting to see what stories come out of the brainstorming activity because students quickly identify their most intense emotional experiences.

6. **SCEDS Lesson Five: Dialogue–Bringing Scenes to Life with Dialogue, Blocking and Emotion.**

    This lesson is fun for students because by this time they will have the confidence to use all of the SCEDS elements to paint an entire short scene.

7. **Your Narrative Scene, SETTING (Brainstorming Chart).**

    Using the skills they have just practiced, writers will place themselves in-the-moment of the scene they are writing. If writers begin here, it's easier to stay in-scene as they continue. Some writers will have only one setting, but many will have more than one. Help them brainstorm the primary location from which the rest of the story unfolds and work with that until it is established. When it is time to go to the flashback or the next setting, your writers will transition with more ease. (With some groups, this is the only chart I use from the "Your Narrative Scene" section; others need the additional help to transition from the practice concepts to the actual scene-writing.)

8. **Your Narrative Scene, CHARACTER (Brainstorming Chart).**

    Using the skills they have just practiced, writers will be able to paint their own characters into their stories with vivid detail.

9. **Your Narrative Scene, EMOTIONS (Brainstorming Chart).**

   Using the skills they have just practiced, writers will be able to identify and write about strong emotional responses within their scenes.

10. **Your Narrative Scene, DIALOGUE & EMOTIONAL RESPONSE (Brainstorming Chart).**

    Writing one small scene successfully will spark students' ideas about where to add dialogue in their own scenes.

Part Two (B): Polishing the SCEDS

For extended work on the SCEDS elements, the following lessons work really well to solidify what was learned in the basic lessons:

1. SCEDS Lesson Two (B): Blending Setting Descriptions into Narratives

2. SCEDS Lesson Three (B): Blending Character Descriptions into Narratives

3. SCEDS Lesson Four (B): Adding Emotional/Physical Response

4. SCEDS Lesson Five (B): Bringing Scenes to Life with Dialogue, Blocking and Emotion

Part Three: Write the First Final Draft

Using their "Your Narrative Scene" charts and written responses, students will be able to begin piecing together their scenes with confidence.

Part Four: Edit First Final Drafts

At times, I use the Part Two (B) SCEDS lessons at this editing stage if I didn't get the chance before. However, I always save the following lesson for the final edit:

1. SCENE CONSTRUCTION Lessson One: Using Flashbacks to Sequence Events in a Scene

2. SCENE CONSTRUCTION Lesson Two: Sequencing Events in a Scene

3. SCENE CONSTRUCTION Lesson Three: Engaging the Reader

    If I teach this lesson too early, students get confused and are hesitant to write. When I teach it after the first draft, lights go on quickly regarding how to make their leads more compelling.

Part Five: Final Drafts/Sharing

I usually hold class readings at the end of this unit, and am always surprised by how many decide to share their stories. I place a stool and a lamp in front of the class – and bring cookies –and invite them to come up to read when "the spirit moves" them. I never require this, but many decide to take that step when they witness the courage of their peers (sometimes a little extra credit is highly motivating, too). These readings have been the highlight for many of my classes. (If students are writing deep, painful stories of abuse, I am especially careful about inviting them to read. By the end of this process, our counselors are aware of the students who are writing about traumatic events and have spoken with them about this issue.)

CURRICULUM GUIDE TO COMMON CORE STATE STANDARDS:
NARRATIVE WRITING

Standard:	Lessons in the *Hippie Boy Teaching Guide* tied to this standard:
CCSS.ELA-Literacy.W.9-10.3d Use precise words and phrases, telling details, and sensory language to convey a vivid picture of the experiences, events, setting, and/or characters.	SCEDS Lesson One: Identifying Sensory Details SCEDS Lesson Two: Painting a Portrait with Words SCEDS Lesson Three: Painting a Place with Words
CCSS.ELA-Literacy.W.9-10.3b Use narrative techniques, such as dialogue, pacing, description, reflection, and multiple plot lines, to develop experiences, events, and/or characters.	SCEDS Lesson Four: Adding Dialogue and Blocking to a Scene SCEDS Lesson Five: Writing to Convey the Physical Impact of Emotions
CCSS.ELA-Literacy.W.9-10.3c Use a variety of techniques to sequence events so that they build on one another to create a coherent whole.	SCENE CONSTRUCTION Lesson One: Using Flashbacks to Sequence Events in a Scene SCENE CONSTRUCTION Lesson Two: Sequencing Events in a Scene
CCSS.ELA-Literacy.W.9-10.3a Engage and orient the reader by setting out a problem, situation, or observation, establishing one or multiple point(s) of view, and introducing a narrator and/or characters; create a smooth progression of experiences or events.	SCENE CONSTRUCTION Lesson Three: Engaging the Reader

DEFINITIONS

Narrative Writing

Narrative writing tells others the stories of our personal experiences and places them within the context of a larger theme, such as a lesson learned.

SCEDS

SCEDS are the building blocks used to create vivid narrative stories. Good narrative writing techniques invite readers to enter into our experience with us and can be broken down into the following five elements:

S—SETTING

C—CHARACTER

E—EMOTIONS

D—DIALOGUE

S—SENSORY DETAILS (sprinkled into all of the above elements)

NARRATIVE SCENES USING SCEDS

Assignment: Write a three-to-five page scene from your life—a piece that begins to reveal the story within your life story. Use the following SCEDS and Structural Elements to make your scene come to life:

_____1. Setting

- When and where does the scene take place?

- What is the environment like?

- What sensory details can you use to describe it?

_____2. Character

- What do your characters look, smell and sound like?

- What are your characters wearing?

- What are the ages of your characters?

- What are your characters' personality characteristics (loud, quiet, assertive)?

- What are your characters' backgrounds?

_____3. Emotional/physical response

- How do you feel during this scene?

- What happens to you physically when you experience these feelings?

- What is going on inside your head during this scene (your thoughts or inner dialogue)?

_____4. Dialogue

- What are you and your characters saying in your scene?

- What are you and your characters doing while you are talking? (blocking)

- What kind of body language is being used?

_____5. Sensory Details (sprinkled into all of the above)

- Visual (what you see)

- Auditory (what you hear)

- Kinesthetic (body language)

- Smell/Taste

SCENE CONSTRUCTION ELEMENTS

When writing your scene, also remember to keep these structural elements in mind.

_____1. Story Arc

- What happens in your story that takes a reader from point "a" to point "b"

- What message do you want the reader to take away?

_____2. Compelling Opening Sentence

- What sentence will immediately grab readers and pull them into your story?

- Does your opening section have action?

_____3. Conflict/Action

- What is the conflict/action in your scene?

- What happens that sets your scene in motion? Does someone get into a fight? Do you get in trouble with an adult?

_____4. Context/backstory/flashback

- What is the context of this scene?

- What paragraphs add necessary background information for the present action to make sense?

- Are there any flashbacks?

_____5. Ending

- What is the conclusion to your scene that makes a satisfactory ending?

- Do you learn a lesson? Do you make a decision?

- Do you come to an understanding?

WRITING PROMPTS

Where were you born and what is your family background/heritage?

What are your interests? What are you most passionate about?

What is most unique about you?

What is your plan for the future?

Describe each member of your family using only one word.

What word would you use to describe yourself?

Which member of your family are you closest to and why?

Which member do you have most trouble with and why? Give an example.

What do you think is your best quality? Give an example.

What do you need to work on?

What makes you really happy?

If you could relive any one day in your entire past, which one would it be and why? Describe that day—who were you with, what were you doing, where were you and why it was so special.

In what way is the true you different from the image people have of you?

What is your greatest insecurity?

What makes you really angry?

Describe a time when someone said or wrote something hurtful about you. Why do you think they did it?

Describe a time when you've been bullied—or have been the bully. (Adults count!)

What are you most afraid of?

In what ways have you tried to escape your life?

How have drugs and alcohol impacted your life?

What is the most painful thing you've ever dealt with—the thing that changed you as a person, which influenced who you are today?

You have three wishes. You can have ANYTHING EXCEPT more wishes. How would you use them?

Describe your ideal future 20 years from now. Where are you living, with whom, what are you doing?

What would you most like to know about your future?

What are you most grateful for?

In most cases, students' story ideas will spring from their answers to the questions regarding what event most changed them, what event was most painful or difficult or what event formed who they are today.

Pre-writing Lesson: Broken Necks and Blank Minds

Objective: Students will begin to understand the importance of "painting a clear picture with words" for their readers.

Lesson set-up: A projector is required, as well as an assortment of interesting pictures. (Pictures that work best for this activity are simple yet interesting ones: a silhouette of a cat next to a broken glass or a dog dressed in a suit.) This lesson works best if your room has individual tables/desks, but can be adapted to any seating arrangement. Place blank sheets of paper and pencils on each table, and assign students into pairs. Tell them to face each other—one facing the front (Describers) and one facing the back wall (Drawers).

1. Tell your students "Your readers' minds are blank; they have no idea what your experience was. It is up to you to paint what happened well so they can experience it with you. Today we are going to mimic this experience through the use of some visuals."

2. Tell the students who are facing the back wall (Drawers): "You have broken necks and blank minds (You cannot turn around, and your mind is completely empty, like a clean slate).

3. Tell students who are facing the screen (Describers), "Your responsibility is to describe the picture on the screen to your partner so that he/she can draw it correctly. You, as "describers," are not allowed any hand motions—no pointing or gesturing—you may only use words."

4. Tell the (Drawers), "You may not ask questions—even for clarification –and you may not use hand gestures, either. Your job is to draw, according to the description that your partner provides."

5. When the Drawers are facing the back, project a picture on the screen for the Describers to see. Provide between 6-8 minutes for describing/drawing. Give warnings regarding how much time they have ("Two minutes left...") and when the time is up, tell the Drawers that they can turn around to see the actual picture. Have students sign their drawings (with both names) and turn them in. My students love to see each other's drawings under the overhead projector. After viewing (and laughing) at the pictures, discuss the experience of both sides. Tie the concept of writing to this activity: "Readers don't know anything about your lives. It is your responsibility to 'paint' your story so that they are engaged and have enough (but not too much) detail to become involved."

6. Have partners switch spots and then repeat the activity.

SCEDS Lesson Plans

SCEDS Lesson One: The Basics—Writing with Sensory Details

Objective: Students will write about a place using sensory details.

1. Give your students a setting and the sensory details observation chart.

   This lesson can be used in limitless situations. I have had them write about my classroom, about the hallway and about our school's courtyard on a nice day. It doesn't matter what setting you choose. This activity will help students gain confidence about their ability to write about any place—no matter how ordinary.

2. Allow students a fixed amount of time just to sit, observe and record details (at least ten minutes). The longer they focus on the sensory details around them, the better their writing will be.

3. When the time limit for observing is up, have them write a paragraph describing the setting.

   Because I usually take my students to a place outside of my classroom, the note-taking and writing activities are completely separate. When we return to the room, I have them write about the observed place for at least ten minutes and I suggest that they try to use at least three details from each column. They can use more or less or none from a column, depending on their own feeling. They should not be concerned with spelling or punctuation, just with words.

4. After at least ten minutes of silent writing, I ask for volunteers to read.

   Usually I have many volunteers, but if I don't, I offer extra credit and then they will read for sure.

5. Ask students to reflect on their writing.

   Since their paragraphs will sound like poetry, it is a good idea to have them reflect on what made their writing good so that the use of descriptive detail is affirmed.

   Julie's response - written from observations made in our school courtyard:

   As I sit on this rough old picnic table, I take in a deep breath and inhale the clean scent of Mathew's cologne. I feel cool gusts of wind glide across the inch of skin that is exposed from my shirt raising up my back. While looking at my surroundings, I notice the dry, brown grass, the cloudless blue sky, and the hot sun shining down on me. I feel warm and cozy. The loose hairs from my ponytail brush against the skin on my face and tickles me.

   Trent's response – written from the same place:

   As I sit on this picnic table, the hot sun beats against my face and the cold wind blows against me. The pine trees stand tall and proud as the leaves rustle in the wind. The hum of the generator and the sound of the plane flying above drown out the words of the people talking by the buses. There are spider webs in the corner of the green arches next to the tan brick wall. The grass is brown, and the leaves are falling slowly from the trees. It smells like fall and clean air. My papers fly off the table as a gust of wind flows through.

Name_____

SCEDS Lesson One —Writing with Sensory Details

Identifying Sensory Details (SCEDS)

1. Directions: Make a note of everything you experience with your five senses. Take note of how to describe what you see and the feel of the ground beneath you and the air around you:

sight	sound	taste/smell	touch

2. On another sheet of paper, write a paragraph describing the surroundings you observed using the above details.

SCEDS Lesson Two: Setting—Painting a Place with Words

Objective: Students will describe a setting using sensory details.

1. Project a picture of a setting. Settings that generate the best descriptions for me are pictures of "haunted" places: an abandoned amusement park, a haunted house, a road to nowhere or a deserted hospital. If possible, include sound to accompany the picture—a suspenseful, scary soundtrack for a haunted place, or the sound of a snowboarder hitting snow for a winter sport picture.

2. Ask the class to offer words to describe each sensory detail separately and tell them they must write down at least three words in each column.

   Example—haunted house, sound category: crunching of leaves, wind rustling the trees, squeaky steps leading to the house, a mouse scurrying across the path.

   Go slowly and wait for the class to offer at least five or six descriptive words before you move onto the next one. This part usually takes at least fifteen minutes.

3. Repeat 1 & 2 with another setting.

4. Ask students to write themselves into one of these scenes using the sensory details from the chart. Allow them at least ten minutes of silent writing time and suggest that they include details from each column.

5. Ask for volunteers to read.

6. Ask students to reflect on the strategies that made their descriptions come alive.

   Tristan's response – written after identifying sensory details in a picture of an abandoned amusement park:

   I walk into the amusement park and I see an old, rusty Ferris wheel. I feel scared because the Ferris wheel squeaks as the wind whistles through the dead trees. The cold air hits my face and it sends a chill down my spine. I take a deep breath and smell rusted metal and old, rotten food. I see a popcorn maker with empty bags sitting beside it. I can feel the broken concrete through my shoes as I run over and jump up on the platform. The rats run out from under the warped wood. I look through the broken fence and see a large piece of metal. I go over to get a closer look and realize that it's a piece of a rollercoaster seat. Another chill runs down my spine.

   Grace's response – written after identifying sensory details in a picture of a snowy field surrounded by pine trees at night:

   It's finally winter and I wake up at 4 am to look outside. I see that it has snowed a lot, so I decide to stay awake and celebrate the fact that nobody is up. I finally get to soak in and enjoy the quiet, perfectly laid out snow I see in my yard. I make a cup of coffee with French Vanilla creamer. I put a long trench coat on that covers my blue flannel pajama pants and my Deathnote t-shirt. I walk outside with my coffee and feel free inside when I see how the straight and sparkly snow lights up the darkness, but of course the coldness instantly hits my face. I hold my coffee tightly since it is the only warmth I have and walk out into the snow, feeling sad that I just ruined its perfection. I ignore it and take a sip of my sweet coffee. I feel the wetness soak into my socks and shoes and decide to ignore it, too. I love the smell of the wet pine trees, which are loaded with snow. This is the best time of the year.

MacKenzie's response – written after identifying sensory details in a picture of an old, abandoned castle on a hill surrounded by fog:

As I walk up the wet, crumbly stairs I slip and quickly grab onto whatever I can to keep myself from falling off the side of the mountain. Looking down I can't see anything except for thick, smoke-like fog and some confused birds trying to fly through. Their caws echo off the eroded brick building. I quickly run inside to escape the raindrops slapping the back of my neck and the smell of mildew and dust hits my nostrils. Even though the rotting floral furniture makes the room feel less empty, the hairs on my arms stand up. "Someone's here with me," I think to myself as I hear a squeak from the hallway.

Kiana's response – written after identifying sensory details in a picture of a hammock sitting in the middle of clear blue water:

I lay in my hammock, floating above the crystal clear water. It's so clear and light blue it looks like someone filtered the whole ocean. I gaze at the sky and let my body hang – feeling the strings push into my skin - while I watch the birds soar around the sun and disappear. I feel the mist of the water as I look over and see a small island across the shore with one palm tree and a man cooking fish. Dark clouds are approaching, overtaking the fluffy white ones above me. When I smell the spices behind me, I know it's time to go in and eat.

Name_____

SCEDS Lesson Two—Writing with Sensory Details

SETTING: PAINTING A PLACE WITH WORDS (**SCEDS**)

1. Describe the setting in the picture using the sensory details chart below (try to brainstorm at least three descriptions for each column):

Visual	Auditory	Feel/Touch	Smell/Taste

2. Describe setting #2:

Visual	Auditory	Feel/Touch	Smell/Taste

3. On another sheet of paper, use the sensory details from your chart to write yourself into either setting #1 or setting #2. Use details from each column.

SCEDS Lesson Two (B): Blending Setting Descriptions into Narratives

Objective: Students will learn how to describe settings effectively within their narratives.

1. Read Eli Peterson's excerpt from "Repressed" or Kayla Kinnard's excerpt from "Sticks and Stones."

2. Instruct students to circle all of the sensory details used to describe the setting —all references to sight, sound, smell, taste and touch.

3. Clarify which words should be circled by marking the passages under a document camera.

4. Tell students to re-write these sections without using any of these details, which will strip them down to basic (boring) sentences.

5. Invite students to read their stripped-down versions of these excerpts out loud. Discuss the differences in the picture painted for the reader.

Name_____

SCEDS Lesson Two (B):

Blending Setting Descriptions into Narratives

Effective descriptions paint vivid pictures in our minds. In this activity, our goal is to take vivid writing and reduce it to dull writing by extracting the life (sensory details) out of it.

Directions:

Step One: Circle all of the sensory details used to describe the setting in the excerpts below—circle all references to sight, sound, smell, taste and touch.

Excerpt from

"Repressed"

by Eliaud Peterson (from *Behind Closed Doors: Stories from the Inside Out*)

Sitting at the end of the cold, hard bed I stare at the wall. I want to leave but the nurses' eyes are on my door. The familiar smell of acidic hospital disinfectant fills my nose and makes me choke. I shift in the giant paper napkin, goose bumps rising on my skin from the cool air pumped into the room. I feel naked anyway, because I was stripped of everything "potentially dangerous" when I was admitted. I pull on my gown and try to cover my legs, but I know they have seen them and I don't like that. I don't let anyone see my scars.

A short, chubby male nurse walks in and says, "Do you want something to eat, sweetie? You're looking thin. You need to keep your strength up."

I ignore him. *Don't call me "sweetie,"* I think. *I don't know you.* My mind drifts through the fog of my day as my chest stirs in rhythm with the heart monitor next to me.

Excerpt from

"Sticks and Stones"

by Kayla Kinnard (from *We Are Absolutely Not Okay*)

I hear glasses being thrown against the walls. The loud noise of my father's rage wakes me from my sleep. I am nine years old and it is the night of New Year's Eve. The clock reads 11:00 p.m. I rip the covers off my sweating body and walk to my bedroom door. My heart feels like it is going to rip out of my chest and I don't know if I feel anger or fear. My adrenaline is through the roof, but it takes a good ten minutes to convince myself to open the door. I hear my parents arguing, but I can't make out the words. I eventually turn the knob and walk out toward the living room. I can see the destruction that my father has caused. This is a daily occurrence in my house. The walls are dripping and stained with the remains of filled glass mugs that have been smashed against the walls. Glass lies in shards across the floor. I see my mother standing in the living room and my father standing in the kitchen. I don't really know what the fight is about, but I am sure it is unimportant. It always is.

Step Two: Re-write these passages without using **any** of the sensory details circled.

SCEDS Lesson Three: Character—Painting a Portrait with Words

Objective: Students will describe a character using sensory details.

1. Project a picture of a "character" on your overhead screen (the more interesting the person is, the better).

2. Ask the class to offer words to describe each sensory detail separately and tell them they must write down at least three words in each column.

    Example: sight —olive skin, grey hair, bowler's hat, wrinkles at the corner of the eyes.

    Go slowly and wait for the class to offer at least five or six descriptive words before you move onto the next column. This part usually takes at least ten minutes.

3. Repeat 1-3 with a different character.

4. On another sheet of paper, ask students to write themselves into a scene where they meet one of the characters they have just described. Allow at least ten minutes for silent writing and suggest that they include details from each column.

5. After at least ten minutes of silent writing, I ask for volunteers to read their descriptions.

6. Ask students to reflect on the strategies that made their descriptions come alive.

Kendra's response – written from the sensory details observed from a picture of an older, wrinkled man wearing a blue golf hat and smoking a cigar:

I hurried back to the restaurant since I forgot my bag there when I closed up. I put my key into the keyhole and turned it. When I opened the door, the smell of cigar smoke hit me. "That's weird," I thought. "No one has been in here for hours." I walked around the counter to retrieve my bag when something blue caught my eye – it was popping up from a booth in the far corner of the restaurant. I grabbed the pepper spray out of my bag and cautiously approached the booth. I stared directly into the blue filmy eyes of a man who appeared to be in his late sixties. I noticed the wrinkles around his mouth as he smiled at me, while smoke rose from his cigar. I wanted to ask him who he was, but my fear would not allow words to come out. He seemed to be a phantom, or some kind of hallucination.

Aaron's response – written from the sensory details observed from a picture of a fair-skinned, dark-haired girl with icy grey eyes:

Her smoky grey eyes, translucent skin and dark, short hair make her look like someone out of a fairy tale. As she walks by, a strong scent of cherry blossoms hits me. She's wearing a striped shirt, skirt and high heels, and her heels click against the pavement to the rhythm of her sway. She looks at me and I want to talk to her, but I can't. I see the lights of the street reflected in her eyes as she continues on.

Name_____

SCEDS Lesson Three—Writing with Sensory Details

CHARACTER: PAINTING A PORTRAIT WITH WORDS (SCEDS)

1.　Describe the character in the picture using the sensory details chart below (try to brainstorm at least three descriptions for each column):

Visual What does this person look like? Describe clothing, approximate age and possible occupation.	**Auditory** How does this person talk? Any other noises associated with him/her?	**Kinesthetic** Describe body language, mannerisms and habits.	**Smell** What odors might you associate with this person?

2.　Describe Character #2:

Visual What does this person look like? Describe clothing, approximate age and possible occupation.	**Auditory** How does this person talk? Any other noises associated with him/her?	**Kinesthetic** Describe body language, mannerisms and habits.	**Smell** What odors might you associate with this person?

3.　On another sheet of paper, use the sensory details from your chart to write yourself into a scene with either character #1 or character #2. Use details from each column.

SCEDS Lesson Three (B):   Blending Character Descriptions into Narratives

Objective: Students will learn how to describe characters effectively within their narratives.

1. Read directions for blending character descriptions into narratives.

2. Discuss the descriptions listed.

3. Instruct students to rewrite the basic narrative(s) by adding character descriptions.

4. Invite them to read their rewrites out loud to the class, and discuss the flow of the writing. Ask students if they are able to "see" the character with these additions.

5. Read the excerpts from both student stories.

Name_____

SCEDS Lesson Three (B):

Blending Character Descriptions into Narratives

It's a very delicate balance between adding "not enough" and "too much" description for characters in your scene. If he/she is a main character, then you will want to use more descriptors—less if the character is secondary, and maybe none if the character is mentioned only once. Refrain from making long lists of traits; instead, blend the descriptions into the narrative so that it flows naturally.

Using the two student examples below, rewrite the sections on another piece of paper and include the descriptions into the flow of the narrative.

1. Brinnon Hall, "Lost Respect"

    a. Brinnon's SCEDS character brainstorming to describe his dad:

    buzzed hair
    muscular
    biceps look like miniature boulders underneath his skin
    golden hazel eyes
    deep smile lines
    pockmarks all over his cheeks from years of popping pimples
    abs feel like rocks when he pulls me in for a hug

    b. Blend the above descriptions into the following narrative:

    After we get past the metal detectors of both steel doors controlled by the guards, we have to walk up to another guard who tells us where to sit while we wait for my dad to get strip searched before he finally walks out.

    I spot him from the line of prisoners as soon as he steps through the door. He checks in with the guard and then walks over to us. He sits down in the chair with the taped yellow stripe on it.

    "So, how have you been, B? What happened to your face?" he says, motioning to my black eye and bloody nose.

2. Jaycee Schrenk, "Stained"

    a. Jaycee's SCEDS character brainstorming to describe her mom:

    High-pitched voice
    Dark-washed blue jeans
    White flowing tank top, white flip flops to match
    Fingers full of diamond rings
    Coach bracelets, ruby red earrings
    Always kissed me on the forehead

    b. Blend the above descriptions into the following narrative:

    "Baby girl, you are my princess, so that means I am the queen. And your father? He's nothing more than a bank account," my mom said as she hopped out of our silver Saab. I watched her walk to the cash machine and return to the car with stacks of hundred dollar bills—money to take me summer clothes shopping.

Excerpt from

"Lost Respect"

by Brinnon Hall (from *Behind Closed Doors: Stories from the Inside Out*)

After we get past the metal detectors of both steel doors controlled by the guards, we have to walk up to another guard who tells us where to sit while we wait for my dad to get strip searched before he finally walks out.

I spot him from the line of prisoners as soon as he steps through the door. His hair is buzzed, like usual, and he is extremely muscular. His biceps look like miniature boulders underneath his skin. He has golden hazel eyes, deep smile lines, and deep pockmarks all over his cheeks from years of popping pimples.

He checks in with the guard and then walks over to us. His abs feel like rocks up against my stomach when he pulls me in for one of his bear hugs. He sits down in the chair with the taped yellow stripe on it.

"So, how have you been, B? What happened to your face?" he says, motioning to my black eye and bloody nose.

Excerpt from

"Stained"

by Jaycee Schrenk (from *Behind Closed Doors: Stories from the Inside Out*)

"Baby girl, you are my princess, so that means I am the queen. And your father? He's nothing more than a bank account," my mom said in her high-pitched voice as she hopped out of our silver Saab. I watched her walk to the cash machine in her dark-washed destroyed blue jeans and white flowing tank top with white flip-flops to match. I knew my mom was beautiful for her age; her style was plain, yet flashy. Her fingers were full of diamond rings, her wrists glinted with Coach bracelets, and ruby red earrings dangled off her ears. She returned to the car with stacks of hundred dollar bills—money to take me summer clothes shopping.

We ran up and down the mall from store to store, my hands holding multiple shopping bags. I felt as if my head was about to explode from the thrill of getting whatever my heart desired. I knew that most 6th graders in my class could never do this. I also knew that my mom had a bad problem with money and our monthly shopping trips were a secret between us. I always felt guilty but my dad rarely ever noticed.

As I placed my stacks of clothes on the Pac Sun counter, I shot a guilty glance at my mom to make sure it was OK to buy everything I wanted. But she reassured me with a kiss on my forehead and handed the cashier four hundred dollar bills.

SCEDS Lesson Four: Emotional/Physical Response

Objective: Students will learn how to describe the physical impact of emotions.

Note: It is especially important to emphasize the physical feeling (heart racing, nose twitching) rather than more emotional descriptions (When I felt fear I felt like I was never going to get to the other side.) It is also fun to compare physical responses between students. When feeling fear, some people's teeth chatter while others feel tingly all over.

1. Project pictures to elicit the feeling of each emotion. Some of the best pictures can be found through either Reuters or the New York Times (best of year photos) because they capture events that are filled with so much expression.

2. Go through each column slowly, asking students to volunteer how they experience each emotion physically. Usually, I have to direct students toward stating the physical feeling, rather than stating another emotion. This class brainstorming time will allow most students to come up with their own answers.

3. Ask students to write about a time they experienced one of these emotions using the physical details they have brainstormed in their charts. Allow them at least ten minutes of silent writing time.

4. Ask for volunteers to read scenes out loud.

5. Ask students to reflect on the strategies that made their descriptions come alive.

Santino's response – written after identifying his physical reaction when he feels anger:

I feel my heart beat faster as my body receives adrenaline. Blood rushes to my face as it gets warm. My hands are shaking out of control as my breathing gets really heavy. All I can think about is how I am going to hurt him. My body can't seem to stop moving.

Martin's response – written after identifying his physical reaction when he feels the thrill of adrenaline:

As I walk up the stairs to get on the Ring of Fire, my palms start to sweat. My heart is beating ten times faster than normal. I start to picture my seatbelt ripping off and me slipping off my seat and I feel like my insides are going to come out. There are over a thousand people around me, but all I can focus on are the noises of the rollercoaster's wheels. I'm getting so light-headed that I feel I can float away like a balloon filled with helium. "Martin! Hurry, it's almost our turn!" I look up and see a beautiful girl with amazing hair and bomb lips. I swear, every time I see her I melt. Then I remember, Oh, that's why I'm getting on this thing!

Destanee's response – written after identifying her physical reaction when she feels anger:

I'm sitting in my room looking at the folded up note from my father. My hands begin to scrunch into fists and I feel my fingernails dig into my sweaty palms. I open one hand to feel my face – it's beet red, so hot, like magma. I open the letter slowly and hair stands up on the back of my neck. When I swallow, it feels like a razor blade is scratching the back of my throat.

Name_____

SCEDS Lesson Four: Emotional/Physical Response

EMOTIONS: WRITING TO CONVEY THE PHYSICAL IMPACT OF EMOTIONS (SCEDS)

1. For each emotion listed, use concrete details to describe how the emotion feels to you physically:

Emotions:	What happens to your body physically when you feel this emotion?
Thrill/Adrenaline Rush	
Anger/Rage	
Fear/Anxiety	
Sadness/Despair	
Joy/Happiness	

2. On another sheet of paper, choose one scenario to describe. Use all elements of SCEDS, if possible, but especially focus on your emotions and how you experience them physically.

Name_____

SCEDS Lesson Four (B): Adding Emotional/Physical Response

Directions: Cross out all emotional/physical responses, and read the excerpts without them. Discuss the difference.

Excerpt from

"Loser, Failure, Dumbass"

by Maize Phillips (from *Behind Closed Doors: Stories from the Inside Out*)

"Hey guys, look! There's Maize! The class retard!" Kristopher Clayman screams out loud enough for me to hear two blocks away. The laughter surrounding him drowns him out for a moment. "Do you think he'll ever be smart enough to know that he might as well just die because he's so fucking worthless?"

Kris has been doing this for the entire school year. My hands are clenched into fists and I want to cover his face in scars. I want to destructively injure him, but leave him alive just so I can make him suffer more. I want to burn his skin off with my rage and break out his teeth with my fists. I am shaking with anger and I think I am going to lose control.

Excerpt from

"The Monster within Him"

by Marika Evenson (from *Behind Closed Doors: Stories from the Inside Out*)

The news anchor appears on the TV screen with the words "child rape arrest" and a picture of handcuffs above him. My stomach is in my throat.

"A man already convicted once of child rape is now suspected of raping another child, and KIRO7 reporter Amy Clancy has dug up the details. She's live downtown where the suspect just went before a court," he says. My hands are clammy as I rub them up and down on my tense, trembling knees.

The screen flashes to a wrinkled blonde woman. "Forty-two year old Jeffrey Evenson is a Level Three sex offender. According to these documents, he has raped again. His alleged victim—a then six-year-old girl," she says and my heart evaporates into thin air.

I see multiple mug shots of my father, and even though I'm disgusted to have the same last name as him, I'm thinking that the reporter could at least pronounce it correctly.

Then the real news begins.

"He was convicted in 1990 for child rape, in 1998 for child molestation and he was convicted twice for failing to register as a sex offender. On Tuesday, he was arrested again in Seattle for allegedly raping a now nine-year-old girl after the girl's father called police."

My ears turn off, my eyes blur and I feel a heavy pressure in my chest.

SCEDS Lesson Five: Dialogue—Bringing Scenes to Life with Dialogue, Blocking and Emotion

Objective: Students will learn how to add dialogue and emotional response to increase the action in their narrative scenes.

1. Project pictures that will elicit an emotional response from students. Almost any picture will work as long as it involves an interesting looking person in it. I have found some great "dialogue-provoking" pictures through Reuters and the New York Times "Best of Year" photos. Some examples: two people on a rollercoaster, screaming, with hands straight in the air; an older man, soaking wet, holding a lobster in his bare hands; a girl "rooftopping" over a cityscape. This is also a good way to involve students in current events; they can imagine themselves talking to people in situations all over the world.

2. Go through each column slowly and ask students to place themselves there, saying "What are you saying? What is he/she saying back to you? What is he/she doing while talking? How do you feel?" Instruct students to fill in the chart while the whole class brainstorms.

3. Once the chart is complete, tell students to choose one scenario to write about, using all of the details they have brainstormed. Allow students to write silently for at least ten minutes.

4. Ask for volunteers to read scenes out loud.

5. Ask students to reflect on the strategies that made their descriptions come alive.

Shelby's response, written after brainstorming dialogue from a picture of two people on a rollercoaster:

She stands at the front of the line, the wind carrying her fiery red hair; it flows back and forth around her face. You can tell she's nervous by the way her palms are sweating while she grips my hand, her grip getting tighter and tighter the closer we get to the rollercoaster.

"Shelby, you know I'm scared of rollercoasters, I don't think I'm ready for this, do you see how far up it goes?" She bites her bottom lip and her face starts to get red.

"Madison, you'll be fine, I know it's scary but I'll be here with you and you can even hold my hand if you want," I say to her. I love riding rollercoasters, the thrill of getting whipped around in a little cart, barely strapped in. My adrenaline starts running as we sit down in the little cart. The rollercoaster attendant comes to our cart dressed in a vest with the rollercoaster's name written in cursive.

He speaks in a monotone voice and pops his gum as he gives instructions. Madison and I pull the bar down as close at it will get to our legs, the cold metal waking up the skin under the bar. The track starts clicking as we begin to climb the huge incline in front of us.

"Shelby this is so scary!" Madison screams. My stomach drops as we start down the incline; I let out a scream and throw my hands up in the air, my body getting thrown into the wall of the cart and then thrown into Madison's side.

"AHHHHH, WOOHOOO!" Madison and I both scream together. We go around a loop and they suspend us upside down. My face heats up while the other passengers scream. The rollercoaster makes us

go flying backwards and we finally come to a stop, the bar now warm with how tight we are gripping it. It flies up and lets us free. I get up and my legs feel like Jell-O, but my grin widens as I help Madison stand up.

"We should go on the bigger one next!" she says excitedly.

Name_____

SCEDS Lesson Five: Dialogue—Bringing Scenes to Life with Dialogue, Blocking and Emotion

1. **DIALOGUE** (SCEDS): Add dialogue, blocking and emotional response to the following scenarios:

Describe the scene	What is said?	Blocking: What are you and _____ doing while you are talking?	What is your emotional response?
	You: The person in the picture:	You: The person in the picture:	
	You: The person in the picture:	You: The person in the picture:	

2. On another sheet of paper, choose one of these scenarios to write about using the dialogue, blocking and emotions identified in the chart.

SCEDS Lesson Five (B): Bringing Scenes to Life with Dialogue, Blocking and Emotion

Objective: Students will learn the importance of using dialogue—rather than summary.

1. Read Emma Norton's excerpt from "Sick and Tired of Being Sick and Tired."

2. Read Emma's story again, this time without any dialogue, blocking or emotion. Discuss the difference.

3. Read Joey Reed's excerpt from "A Strife in My Life."

4. Instruct students to re-write this portion of Joey's narrative in the same way that Emma's has been stripped down: to remove all dialogue, blocking and emotion (turn it into summary).

5. Have students share their stripped-down versions. Discuss (and laugh).

Name_____

SCEDS Lesson Five (B): Bringing Scenes to Life with Dialogue, Blocking and Emotion.

Directions:

Step One: Read Emma's excerpt from "Sick and Tired of Being Sick and Tired."

Excerpt from

"Sick and Tired of Being Sick and Tired"

by Emma Norton (from Behind Closed Doors: Stories from the Inside Out)

A tall, thin cop approaches us. I can tell by his muscled arms that he's in good shape. He has a thick mustache and stubble on his jaw. He acknowledges us with that smartass look that cops have, like he's the coolest.

"You know, this is a no trespassing zone," he says.

Sam does the talking and I keep my mouth shut. "Oh, I'm sorry officer. We were just talking and didn't know it was a no trespassing zone." She tries to sound sweet while standing in front of the bong to hide it.

"Please sit down on the edge of the wall," the cop asks with a hint of a demand.

We hesitate for a minute but end up following his direction. He sees the bong shoved into the corner and points to it, giving us a knowing look.

"That was here when we got here," Sam says quickly. "It's not ours. We were just looking at it." I can tell he isn't buying it from his hard eyes staring at us.

"It really isn't ours. There's not even anything in it," Sam says, trying harder to convince him.

He takes it and gives us a look like he isn't stupid. "Okay, well, I'm going to throw it away in that dumpster," he says.

"Wait, can I do it?" Sam asks. I watch her walk to a big green dumpster and toss it in while I'm still sitting on the edge of the wall. I frown at the dumpster and forget about it.

Step Two: Now read Emma's excerpt without dialogue, blocking or emotional response:

A tall, thin cop approaches us. I can tell by his muscled arms that he's in good shape. He has a thick mustache and stubble on his jaw. He acknowledges us with that smartass look that cops have, like he's the coolest. He tells us it's a no trespassing zone and Sam tries to talk herself out of the situation but he tells us to sit down on the edge of the wall. He points to the bong and Sam claims it's not ours. He takes it and gives us a look like he isn't stupid and throws it in the dumpster, but Sam asks if she can do it herself.

Step Three: Read Joey's excerpt below:

Excerpt from

"A Strife in My Life"

by Joey Reed (from *You've Got it All Wrong*)

"What's in your backpack?" he asks.

They always ask me that. Every damn time.

"Um, papers and stuff," I answer.

"Do you have any sharpies in there?" he asks, motioning again to my backpack.

"No, my mom's too poor to get me one," I say, resting my hands on the back of my head.

"So, if I was to go up there and check, there won't be any graffiti on the walls up there then?" he asks, pointing his finger up to the roof.

Yeah, totally. I totally go up there where no one will be able to see anything and make a stupid gang tag that nobody will be able to read anyways. Totally.

"Uh, no. Besides, graffiti's something that all those stupid gangs do!" I state sarcastically.

"What's your name? he asks.

"Oh, it's Caleb," I reply.

He pulls a notepad and pen out of his chest pocket and begins to write something on it. "Okay, Caleb. What's your last name?"

I look up at him, trying to think.

"Uh, it's Caleb Reed," I say.

He wears a nametag, but I don't get to read it fully. I don't like it that he's rushing me; things never turn out well when I am rushed by people.

Step Three: Re-write Joey's excerpt by taking out all of the dialogue, blocking and emotional response.

SCENE CONSTRUCTION Lesson One: Flashbacks

Objective: Students will learn how to place a scene within a scene.

1. Reading scenes that use the flashback technique is a great way to familiarize students with this structure (excerpts from Brayan Hernandez' "Run Up or Shut Up" or Tattiyana Fernandez' "Replaced" are included). After reading the excerpts, I ask students to identify the transition sentences between present and past.

2. For practice: Tell students that they will be writing their own "Three-Paragraph Flashback" – a scene within a scene – and to focus specifically on smooth transitions.

3. Project a picture of an interesting setting. I use one of many pictures I have collected of "abandoned places" because they encourage a lot of imagination: an abandoned amusement park, a military island, a "road to nowhere," an empty house filled with sand.

4. Ask the class to offer words to describe each sensory detail separately and tell them they must write down at least three words in each column (just like they did for SCEDS lesson 2 on setting).

5. PRESENT: Have students write themselves into this setting using the sensory details they have just brainstormed.

6. PAST (FLASHBACK): For their second paragraph, they must transition into the story of how they arrived at this place. (These will get very creative – running from the law, "one wrong turn," a zombie apocalypse, etc.)

7. BACK TO THE PRESENT: For their last paragraph, they must transition their reader back to the present.

8. Ask for volunteers to read their scenes and to identify their transition sentences.

SCENE CONSTRUCTION Lesson One: Flashbacks

Excerpt from

"Run Up or Shut Up"

By Brayan Hernandez (from *We Are Absolutely Not Okay*)

"Don't be scared," my homeboy told me.

I was shaking. Sweat was building between the palm of my hand and the handle of the single action .22 revolver I was holding. I had never held a gun and, being the size that I was, I thought it was really heavy. I felt the pressure in my head, imagining how it could all go wrong. It seemed like the whole world knew what I was about to do and the glares of the few people that walked past terrified me. But I couldn't show any type of weakness. I had to make it seem like I was in control of the situation.

I had received the call that would place me here a couple of days before from one of my homeboys.

"What's good, little homie?" he had said over my cell phone's speakerphone. His ranking was a "Soldier," meaning he was one of many roots that held the gang in place. He had been in the click since it started.

"Nothing," I replied with a rough voice, trying to act tough.

"You down to put in work this weekend? Because there is a meeting set up and your cousin talked about you coming in. It's now or never little homie," he said in a voice that made my heart pump faster.

"Yeah," I mumbled, not wanting to hear or see what was coming next. "Is he going to be there?" I asked. My cousin had been in the gang for a couple months before I joined in and he was already ranked as "Third Word" in the gang, meaning that his words counted when the gang made a decision. We had moved from Mexico City two years earlier when I was ten. Neither of us had known anyone, and we couldn't speak to anyone. The transition was difficult, but through the gang we had found a family who understood what we were going through.

"Na, he says it's your decision and you're on your own. But don't worry. Ain't nothing out of the ordinary. We just going hunting, trying to get some cash. You up for it?" he asked.

"Alright then, I'm down" I said firmly. A feeling of desperation washed over me. I had just given my word and I couldn't let them down.

"Cool, I'll be seeing you little one," he said, and then hung up.

After that call my mind had just two thoughts, to rob or to leave and never step up. If I didn't do this I would never be able to join the gang.

A couple of days later, I was mobbing through the streets of downtown Everett with three other members and a gun, looking for a mark.

"All you got to do is point and ask for everything. If they don't give it up you just take it," one of my homeboys instructed me.

I didn't answer. I knew what I had to do. If it all went bad and the police found me or caught me in the act, I knew I had to keep my mouth shut.

Excerpt from

"Replaced"

By Tattiyanna Fernandez (from You've Got it All Wrong)

Here I stand in a room that I should recognize, but it's completely different. It's not my room. It's not the room that I painted, not the room I slept in just last week. I knew things were going to be different, and I knew I would have to share a room with the baby if it was a girl, which it was. But I didn't know they were going to completely change my room.

My light pink-colored walls, my twin-sized bed, my heart-patterned bed spread, my paintings and posters are all gone. The chandelier my dad put in especially for me, my clothes, my dresser...everything is gone. Just like that. It looks like a full on nursery. Baby clothes, baby toys and a crib. The walls are now purple with lady bugs and butterflies.

Where is all my stuff? Where's my bed? Where's all my art? Where do they expect me to sleep. With the dog? All these thoughts that are screaming and chanting in my head want to come out, but I won't let them. I know it's over. It's the day I know my dad is going to forget all about me.

I feel betrayed. Just weeks before, my step mom and I had a conversation on the phone.

"Hey, are you busy? I know you're getting ready to go camping with Payton but I wanted to ask you something," she said, all chipper-sounding, like usual.

"Alright what's up?" I replied. I was worried because whenever she started a conversation like that, it was something bad.

"Well if the baby is a girl, would it be okay if you guys shared a room? Being it's already girly and stuff?" she asked.

I breathed a sigh of relief.

"Yeah I'd be okay with that, as long and she doesn't cry too much! Ha-ha," I said, tying to joke around.

"Well, she wouldn't sleep there for a few months," she said.

"Oh, well, yeah, if it's a girl I'm totally fine with sharing my room," I said again, happy she had asked me first.

I had been completely fine with sharing my room with her. But when I see my changed room and all my stuff gone, it feels like there is a big rubber ball stuck in my throat. I want to cry, but I can't. Everything is blurry. I am looking at the new lady bug mini-ceiling fan through tears.

Questions for Discussion

1. Where do the flashbacks begin and end?

2. What sentences transition the reader from present to past and back again?

Name_____

SCENE CONSTRUCTION Lesson One: Using Flashbacks to Sequence Events in a Scene

Definition:

flashback(n) - a scene in a story that is set in a time earlier than the main story.

Instructions: Write a three –paragraph scene in which you utilize the flashback technique (place a scene within a scene). You will move from present to past and back to present again. Your goal is to transition between them smoothly.

Paragraph One: PRESENT

Paragraph Two: PAST

Paragraph Three: BACK TO THE PRESENT

1.   Describe the setting in the picture using the sensory details chart below (try to brainstorm at least three descriptions for each column):

Visual	Auditory	Feel/Touch	Smell/Taste

2.   PRESENT: In your first paragraph, place yourself in this setting using these sensory details.

3.   PAST (FLASHBACK): In your second paragraph, transition into the story of how you arrived at this place.

4.   BACK TO THE PRESENT: In your last paragraph, transition back to the present.

SCENE CONSTRUCTION Lesson Two: Sequencing Events in a Scene

Objective: Students will learn how to sequence the events of a scene in order to include the past within the present moment.

1. Read directions for sequencing events in a scene worksheet, then have students read the events out loud for Brayan's scene.

2. Ask students to place events in an order that makes sense.

3. Go over their responses and discuss. Below is how Brayan Hernandez ordered the events in his scene "One Shot" (from You've Got it All Wrong):

__P___ a. ___He picks a fight in the gym with a Blood.

__FB _ b. ___He asks his cousin if he can join, cousin says he's too young.

__FB__ c. ___He asks the shot caller, who says he has to prove he is up for it.

__P____d. ___The fight is broken up and he gets escorted to the principal's office.

4. Repeat for the next three scenes. Answers may differ. The most important take-away from this lesson is that students consider how to place the reader in the moment while including important elements that have previously occurred.

SCENE CONSTRUCTION Lesson Two: Sequencing Events in a Scene

If the parts of a scene take place over a period longer than an hour (over the course of a day, a week or a month), events must be ordered using the flashback technique. Structuring events in this way will ground the story in a time and place and allow your reader to experience the moment with you.

Instructions: Consider the following story events and how you might order them using a flashback scene within the main (present) scene. Remember that the main scene must take place in a relatively short time period (usually under an hour).

Reorder the events in each scene. Place a "P" next to the events in the present, main scene and "FB" next to the events in the flashback.

1. Scene: Brayan wants to join a gang.

    a. He asks his cousin if he can join, cousin says he's too young.

    b. He asks the shot caller, who says he has to prove he is up for it.

    c. He picks a fight in the gym with a Blood.

    d. The fight is broken up and he gets escorted to the principal's office.

___ 1. _____

___ 2. _____

___ 3. _____

___ 4. _____

2. Scene: After Isabel's father disowns her, she tries to reconcile with him.

    a. Isabel's father sees her coming out of an apartment building with her boyfriend.

    b. Later that night he comes into her bedroom, whips her and tells her she is no longer his daughter.

    c. One month later, she tries to reconcile with him.

    d. Her father refuses her request.

___ 1. _____

___ 2. _____

___ 3. _____

___ 4. _____

3.   Scene: Adam gets bullied to the breaking point.

   a. Adam gets bullied on the way to school every day by two boys.

   b. One day they decide to bully him during PE.

   c. He loses control, fights them and gets sent to the principal's office.

___ 1. _____

___ 2. _____

___ 3. _____

4.   Scene: Tatti's room is redecorated for her new baby sister.

   a. Tatti's step mother asks her if she would mind sharing a room with her new baby sister. Tatti agrees.

   b. Weeks later, she sees the room and it's no longer hers. All of her stuff is gone and has been replaced with a crib and baby decorations.

   c. She asks her dad where she should sleep. He suggests the couch.

___ 1. _____

___ 2. _____

___ 3. _____

SCENE CONSTRUCTION Lesson Three: Engaging the Reader

The following excerpts come from *We Are Absolutely Not Okay, You've Got it All Wrong*, and *Behind Closed Doors: Stories from the Inside Out*.

Excerpt from "**A Taste of the Real World**" by Leandra Hall

"Oh come on, baby. I just wanna spend some time with you." The man's deep, low voice sent shivers down my spine. The feeling of his hand rubbing my upper back kept me frozen in fear. "How much will it take?"

Excerpt from "**Run Up or Shut Up**" by Brayan Hernandez

"Don't be scared," my homeboy told me.

I was shaking. Sweat was building between the palm of my hand and the handle of the single action .22 revolver I was holding.

Excerpt from "**Gone**" by Destiny Allison

My heart stopped when I heard my grandma speak the words. As if it wasn't bad enough hearing them the first time, they kept replaying in my head. "We went to your dad's house this morning. He's dead."

Excerpt from "**He Was My Hero**" by Isabel Cordova

It's been eight months since my dad and I have talked to each other. I am ready to confront him, tell him that I am sorry and ask him to forgive me.

Excerpt from "**Good Intentions, Bad Results**" by Shelby Asbury

"When we walk up those stairs, he's going to be there," the prosecutor says as we make our way toward the courtroom.

Excerpt from "**Repressed**" by Eli Peterson

Sitting at the end of the cold, hard bed I stare at the wall. I want to leave but the nurses' eyes are on my door.

1. How does each lead engage you into the action of the scene?

2. How does each lead orient you to the conflict of the story?

SCENE CONSTRUCTION Lesson Three: Engaging the Reader

Objective: Students will learn to engage readers into their stories by presenting the conflict within the first few sentences.

1. Ask students what draws them into a story. What makes them want to read more? How long do they "stick" with a story until they give up on it?

2. Read examples of good leads and ask students what makes each one compelling. Are the leads active? Do they state the conflict clearly?

3. After determining the qualities of a good lead, have them work in pairs to write leads for the examples given.

4. After ten minutes, ask students to share their leads.

5. Discuss each lead. Is it active? Is the conflict clear?

SCENE CONSTRUCTION Lesson Three: Engaging the Reader

To engage your reader from the very first sentence of your story, follow these two simple rules:

1. Begin with action.

2. Make the conflict clear.

Directions: Write a compelling lead for each scene below.

1. You are followed by three bullies on the way home from school. They are picking on you.

_____

_____

_____

_____

2. Police arrive at your house and handcuff you (or someone in your family).

_____

_____

_____

_____

3. You are about to meet your biological father/mother for the first time (or a sibling that you didn't know existed until just recently). You are extremely nervous about the meeting.

_____

_____

_____

_____

It is 11:20 at night, and your curfew, is 11:30 however, you are still 15 minuts a way from home. What could possibly go wrong if you drive over the speed limit.

Name_____

Writing with Sensory Details—Your Narrative Scene

SETTING: PAINTING A PLACE WITH WORDS (**SCEDS**)

1. Choose the real-time setting (usually the first setting) from your narrative scene.

2. Describe this setting using the sensory details chart below (try to brainstorm at least three descriptions for each column).

Visual	Auditory	Feel/Touch	Smell/Taste

3. Use this chart to brainstorm your secondary setting – it may be set within a flashback or another place you move to in real-time.

Visual	Auditory	Feel/Touch	Smell/Taste

4. On another sheet of paper, write a paragraph describing your first setting, then return to your second chart when you get to your next one.

Name_____

Writing with Sensory Details—Your Narrative Scene

CHARACTER: PAINTING A PORTRAIT WITH WORDS (SCEDS)

1. Choose a main character from your narrative scene:_____

2. Describe this person using the sensory details chart below (try to brainstorm at least three descriptions for each column).

Visual What does this person look like? Describe clothing, approximate age and possible occupation.	Auditory How does this person talk? Any other noises associated with him/her?	Kinesthetic Describe body language, mannerisms and habits.	Smell What odors might you associate with this person?

3. What is important for the reader to know about this character's background?

4. On another sheet of paper, write a paragraph describing this person using the above details plus an important fact from the background story.

Name_____

Writing with Sensory Details—Your Narrative Scene

EMOTIONS: WRITING TO CONVEY THE PHYSICAL IMPACT OF EMOTIONS (SCEDS)

1. Identify three emotions experienced during your narrative scene and describe how these emotions feel to you physically:

Event in your narrative scene:	Emotion experienced:	What happened to your body physically when you felt this emotion?

2. On another sheet of paper, choose at least one part of your narrative scene and describe your emotional/physical response to the events that happen.

Name_____

Writing with Sensory Details—Your Narrative Scene

DIALOGUE & **EMOTIONAL** RESPONSE (SCEDS)

1. Choose two events within your narrative and identify dialogue, blocking and your emotional response:

Event	What is said?	Blocking: What are you and _____ doing while you are talking?	What is your emotional response?
	You: _____ :	You: _____ :	
	You: _____ :	You: _____ :	

2. On another sheet of paper, choose one of these events to write about using the dialogue, blocking and emotions identified in the chart.

Transformations

HOW WRITING MY STORY CHANGED MY LIFE

By Carolina Mooney—Author, "Bastard Child"

All my life I've had low self-esteem and tortured relationships with boys. I don't know my father, which has led me to engage in every form of self-destructive behavior possible. I've been promiscuous, constantly cheating on my significant others. I've never had a monogamous relationship that lasted longer than six months. Until now.

Last year, my high school English teacher gave me what I thought was yet another standard high school English assignment—a weekend's worth of work at most.

Boy, was I wrong. When I first wrote my piece, I didn't think much of it. It wasn't until I participated in a live interview on a local television show with two other authors from our book that I understood the full potential of our publication. We had written a self-help book for others while helping ourselves with our own healing process.

I originally decided to use a fake name for my story because I felt like I could hide behind it. The content of my story was extremely personal and graphic and covered things I didn't like to talk about with the closest of friends or even think about really. I was embarrassed and ashamed of my past and I felt that if I used a made up name, I wouldn't have to deal with the reality of the situation. My family knew nothing of the content of my piece other than the obvious part about me not having a father. Even then, they didn't know to which extent the lack of a father figure had affected me.

When my family ended up reading my story at our book release party, I felt violated and their reaction made me wish I hadn't written it. I had told them repeatedly that I didn't want them to read my piece and that if they did, I would be really angry. But how could I expect them not to? They were proud of me for having something published regardless of the content, and they were curious as to why I didn't want them to read it.

Although I was initially pissed off that they had read my story, it laid everything out on the table and forced us to talk about issues that really needed to be brought up. In doing so, it has changed my relationship with my family for the better.

While this experience was really difficult and exhausted me emotionally, if I ever had the chance to do something like this again, I definitely would. It was a great learning opportunity and I know that it has helped me immensely. I now realize that I need to own up to my past —that my past has made me who I am. I'm proud of what I've accomplished and since my secret is out, I no longer need to hide behind a pen name.

It's my hope that my story can continue to help others.

Read Carolina's story in *We Are Absolutely Not Okay: Fourteen Stories by Teenagers Who Are Picking Up the Pieces.*

TAKING DOWN ALL MY WALLS AND DEFENSES

By Leandra Hall—Author, "A Taste of the Real World"

When I first started writing about the time I ran away from home and encountered a man who forcefully begged me to have sex with him for money, the incident had already been on my mind for several weeks. Though four years had passed, I still couldn't get over it. Looking back on it made me feel violated and uncomfortable—sometimes even sending shivers down my back when I thought of it in detail.

I was skeptical about sharing my story at first. The idea that telling your story helps you get it off your chest and makes you feel better sounded like something your mom would say. But I decided to give it a shot and write about it in my English class. Sharing my experience with others was like taking down all of my walls and defenses, and allowing people I barely knew to see the hurt little girl who was hiding inside. At least that's how I felt.

When people started reading my story, they made me feel better about the incident by reminding me of how messed up a man that old must be to desire such a small young girl. They also made me feel good about myself when they praised my storytelling abilities. I'd never felt confident in reading or writing and always considered English my worst subject. But here were these adults and classmates telling me that I was actually good at it. It made me start to really enjoy writing–as long as it's in small portions.

As I stated briefly in my story, I went through a phase in my early teen years when I'd decided I could do whatever I wanted to do and didn't have to listen to my parents. As a result I got into some tangled situations that were pretty hard to get out of. I just want those who feel the same way I once did to realize that by refusing to listen, you can encounter a lot of danger and really get hurt. Rape and kidnapping really do happen. I've had to learn a lot of life's lessons the hard way and the thought of others having to do that is terrifying. I understand that not all may listen. But I hope that by sharing my story, at least a few will get it.

Read Leandra's story in *We Are Absolutely Not Okay: Fourteen Stories by Teenagers Who Are Picking Up the Pieces.*

THE EXPERIENCE OF A LIFETIME AND THE HEALING IT HAS BROUGHT ME

By Marika Evenson—Author, "The Monster within Him"

When Marjie gave us the assignment to write our stories in her English class, I cried. I just wanted to punch her. But after a good cry session, I changed my mind and decided to write mine. It's been very hard, but now I realize that this has been the experience of a lifetime.

I have always had problems with cutting and drugs and it has always tied back to the emptiness I've felt from not having my dad. Through this writing experience, though, I have healed more than I ever could have imagined. I started out hating myself and now have come around to loving myself.

Even though I hate what has happened to me in my life, it has made me who I am and I no longer want to change that. I don't think I would have ever felt that way fully without getting my story out. It has made me feel strong and has given me my power back.

We tell our stories hoping that they can help more than just us. I hope that you, too, will write your story and have your voice heard, because it is the most fulfilling feeling that you can experience.

Read Marika's story in *Behind Closed Doors: Stories from the Inside Out.*

FIGHT BACK METAPHORICALLY

By Maize Phillips –Author, "Loser, Failure, Dumbass"

This experience has helped me not only to understand my own struggles and how to overcome them, but also to understand the importance of not judging anyone by what they do, but instead finding out why they do it. It has helped to let my family know what I've been through, which has brought us even closer. Writing and sharing my story has also helped motivate me to make better decisions and to succeed in school.

The negative motivation that these people gave me was the motivation to prove them wrong. I was tired of being labeled, and I wanted to be heard. When my voice was finally heard, I was overjoyed and was glad that my story could help so many people. People finally looked into my true being rather than discarding me as another teenager or as an idiot.

The writing process was rough. I wrote over twenty drafts total after working on my story for three months. But in the end, it was all worth it because writing and sharing my story has changed my perspective about other people. If anyone is struggling with this same situation, don't fight back physically or verbally; fight back metaphorically. You can do anything if you truly believe that you can, but you have to really believe in yourself. You cannot pretend to believe it. You can do it.

Read Maize's story in *Behind Closed Doors: Stories from the Inside Out.*

FINALLY ACCEPTING WHO I AM

By Brieaunna Dacruz — Author, "Closet Doors"

I learned so much from writing and publishing my story. When I was brainstorming what to write about, at first I didn't want to dwell on my past. But when I finally decided to share my story about coming out, it was one of the best decisions I have ever made. It helped me express what I have gone through in ways I never could before.

If you aren't accepted for who you are by others, don't let them break you. Stand up for yourself and stay strong. Nothing and no one is worth hiding your true identity. Coming out was the best decision I have ever made. It has brought me to where I am today and I couldn't be happier. My future has hope, things have gotten better, and I can now get through any obstacle that gets in my path.

Read Brieaunna's story in *Behind Closed Doors: Stories from the Inside Out.*

  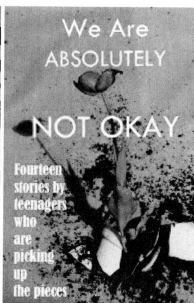

Purchase our books at:

Amazon (eBook/Paperback)
Barnes and Noble.com (Paperback)
Edmonds Book Shop (Paperback)

Please contact us for discounts on class sets.

www.WriteToRight.org

ABOUT MARJIE BOWKER

Marjie Bowker has taught English and a little history somewhere in the world for the past 18 years: in China, Norway and Vietnam, in addition to her "regular" spot at Scriber Lake High School, an alternative high school just north of Seattle, Washington. A strong advocate of community/student partnerships, she is constantly fostering relationships with community leaders to help enrich the lives of the teens she works with and was recently recognized as "Teacher of the Year" by the local VFW chapter for her innovative teaching/mentorship style. Past awards include a Paul Harris Fellowship Rotary Award and two NEH scholarships to study at Columbia University & Crow Canyon Archaeology Center. Marjie has traveled to more than thirty countries and is always on the lookout for creative ways to infuse her love of travel into her teaching career, including leading two trips to Costa Rica to save the Leatherback sea turtles.

ABOUT INGRID RICKS

Ingrid Ricks is the author of The New York Times Bestseller *Hippie Boy*, which was recently acquired by Berkley, a division of Penguin Random House. She is also the author of Focus, a memoir about her journey with the blinding eye disease Retinitis Pigmentosa, and a short story collection, *A Little Book of Mormon (and Not So Mormon) Stories*. She is currently working on a memoir about her yearlong quest to heal her eyesight, and is blogging about her journey at www.determinedtosee.com. Ingrid's essays and stories have been featured on Salon and NPR. Along with writing, she is passionate about leveraging the new world of digital publishing to give teens a voice. For more information, visit: www.ingridricks.com.

CPSIA information can be obtained
at www.ICGtesting.com
Printed in the USA
LVOW03s1923261216
518684LV00007B/73/P